VOLCANO
Earth's Power

David and Patricia Armentrout

Rourke
Publishing LLC
Vero Beach, Florida 32964

9780824914110

www.rourkepublishing.com

PHOTO CREDITS: Cover, pgs 10, 14 inset, 17 inset, 19, 23 courtesy of the U.S. Geological Survey/HVO; Pgs 5, 5 inset, 6 inset, 9, 21, 22, 25, 25 inset, 26 inset, 29 courtesy of the U.S. Geological Survey/CVO; Title pg, pgs 14, 17, 21 courtesy of the U.S. Geological Survey/AVO; Pg 13 courtesy of NASA; Pgs 6, 10, 12, 18, 26 ©Photodisc, Inc.; Pg 20 ©Aschwin Prein; Pg 10 inset ©Armentrout

Title page: Volcanoes can remain quiet for hundreds of years and then erupt without warning.

Editor: Robert Stengard-Olliges

Cover and page design by Nicola Stratford

Library of Congress Cataloging-in-Publication Data

Armentrout, David, 1962-
  Volcanoes / David and Patricia Armentrout.
     p. cm. -- (Earth's power)
  Includes bibliographical references and index.
  1. Volcanoes--Juvenile literature. I. Armentrout, Patricia, 1960- II. Title. III. Series: Armentrout, David, 1962- Earth's power.
QE521.3.A7575 2007
551.21--dc22
                              2006011223

Printed in the USA

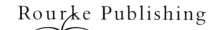

Rourke Publishing
www.rourkepublishing.com – rourke@rourkepublishing.com
Post Office Box 3328, Vero Beach, FL 32964

TABLE OF CONTENTS

Mount St. Helens 4

Ring of Fire 8

An Active Planet 11

Hot Spots 12

A Volcanic Eruption .16

Year without a Summer 20

Deadly Eruptions 24

Yellowstone 27

A Creative Force 28

Glossary 30

Further reading 31

Websites to Visit 31

Index 32

MOUNT ST. HELENS

On May 18, 1980, an early morning explosion rocked southwest Washington State. The blast was thousands of times more powerful than the atomic bomb dropped on Hiroshima, Japan during World War II. Mount St. Helens, a long **dormant** volcano, had re-awakened.

The destructive energy released that day was incredible. Within minutes, more than 200 square miles of forest lay in ruins. An avalanche of rock and mud filled the valleys. Rivers and mountain roads were buried under thousands of tons of volcanic debris. Hot ash and smoke clogged the air. Fifty-seven people were killed along with thousands of animals including bear, elk, and mountain lions.

Mount St. Helens before the 1980 eruption.

Mount St. Helens spews a column of ash and debris during the 1980 eruption.

A scientist collects samples of volcanic ash.

Mount Kilimanjaro, a dormant volcano for almost

200 years, rises 19,340 feet (5,895 meters)

in Tanzania, Africa.

The **eruption** at Mount St. Helens was devastating, but the loss of human life could have been much worse. Fortunately, few people lived near the volcano's danger zone.

There are thousands of volcanoes around the world. About 500 are active. Scientists consider a volcano active if it has erupted during recorded history. Some volcanoes remain quiet for thousands of years, while others erupt frequently. Often the quiet ones are most dangerous.

Volcanologists are scientists that specialize in the study of volcanoes.

RING OF FIRE

Most volcanoes are located along the edges of continents. More than half are within an area that encircles the Pacific Ocean, known as the "Ring of Fire."

1815-Tambora, Indonesia:

The eruption of Tambora was one of the largest in recorded history. Pyroclastic flows flattened nearby villages. Huge clouds of ash darkened the sky for weeks. Nearly 10,000 people died during the initial eruption. At least 80,000 more died from starvation and disease brought about by the complete destruction of the Island's vegetation and food supply.

> 🔥 A pyroclastic flow is an avalanche of hot gas, ash, and fragments of volcanic debris. The deadly avalanche flows at high speed down volcanic slopes.

A pyroclastic flow races down the flanks of Mount St. Helens.

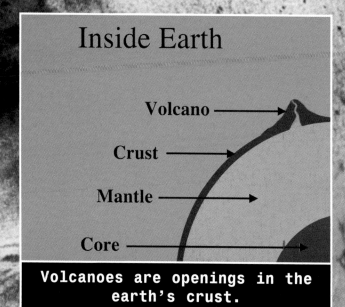

Inside Earth

Volcano ⟶

Crust ⟶

Mantle ⟶

Core ⟶

Volcanoes are openings in the earth's crust.

Lava can reach temperatures of over 2,000 degrees.

AN ACTIVE PLANET

What causes a volcanic eruption? The answer lies deep below the earth's surface. Scientists believe the earth's interior has layers. The outer layer, or **crust**, is made up of huge slabs of rock called **tectonic plates**. The plates float on a hot, semi-**molten** interior layer, called the **mantle**. The mantle rests on the center, or **core**.

Volcanoes are simply openings in the earth's crust that allow molten material from the mantle to escape to the earth's surface. Volcanoes and earthquakes are more common in places where tectonic plates collide, or rub against each other.

Temperatures inside the earth are hot enough to melt rock. Scientists estimate that temperatures range from more than 7,000 degrees Fahrenheit in the core to 2,700 degrees in the mantle. It is hard to imagine that much of the earth is composed of super hot rock, but it helps explain why volcanoes exist.

HOT SPOTS

Not all volcanoes occur near tectonic plate boundaries. Some arise in areas known as hot spots. The volcanoes of Hawaii are a good example. The Hawaiian Islands contain some of the world's biggest and most active hot spot volcanoes. In fact, the entire island chain was created by volcanic activity.

The volcanic islands of Hawaii are known for their beautiful beaches.

Anak Krakatau, meaning "child of Krakatau," grew from the remains of the Krakatau volcano that collapsed in 1883.

Lava cools as it creeps down slope.

Scientists view a volcano from the safety of an airplane.

The largest volcano on earth is Mauna Loa on the Island of Hawaii. From its base on the sea floor, Mauna Loa rises more than 56,000 feet. Most of the giant volcano lies hidden below sea level. Mauna Loa is much taller than Mount Everest, the highest mountain on earth, which stands 29,035 feet above sea level.

Another Hawaiian volcano, Kilauea, is one of the most active volcanoes in the world. Its most recent eruption began in January 1983 and has continued ever since. Lava flows from Kilauea have caused property damage and destroyed homes and highways. Because the flows are slow moving, people are rarely injured.

Mauna Loa is big, but it pales in comparison to the largest volcano in the solar system. Olympus Mons is a huge volcano on Mars. It is roughly the size of the state of Arizona and is nearly 100 times larger than Mauna Loa.

A VOLCANIC ERUPTION

A volcanic eruption starts deep below the earth's surface. Hot molten rock from the mantle slowly begins to rise. It works its way up through cracks in the earth's crust or creates new paths by melting away any solid material in its way. The molten rock, or **magma**, collects in pockets called magma chambers. As a chamber fills and grows, the pressure inside increases. Eventually, the pressure becomes so great that the magma forces its way, sometimes violently, to the surface. Magma, which reaches the surface, is called lava.

The earth's crust, which is up to 42 miles thick, makes up about one percent of the earth's volume. The mantle and the core make up the remaining 99 percent.

16

Scientists take samples from a
pool of extremely hot lava.

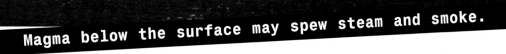

Magma below the surface may spew steam and smoke.

The violent eruption of Mount Pinatubo in 1991 ended 500 years of quiet dormancy.

During major eruptions, volcanoes eject lava, poisonous gas, smoke, ash, and huge chunks of rock hundreds or thousands of feet into the air. After the initial blast, volcanoes may continue to spew ash and lava for months.

Red-hot lava spills from a vent in a Hawaiian volcano.

Mount Pinatubo was a dormant volcano until its fiery eruption in 1991. Numerous earthquakes alerted volcanologists to a potential eruption and thousands of locals were evacuated. A typhoon passing over the island added to the climactic eruption on June 15, 1991. Nearly 300 people died when their roofs collapsed from the weight of heavy, wet ash.

YEAR WITHOUT A SUMMER

AD 79-Mount Vesuvius:

Mount Vesuvius is the only active volcano on the European mainland. Its most famous eruption occurred in AD 79. Multiple tremors and earthquakes were followed by a catastrophic eruption that buried nearby villages including Pompeii and Herculaneum. Several thousand people were killed. The eerily preserved remains were rediscovered hundreds of years later.

Scientists believe large volcanic eruptions can affect weather around the world. Major volcanic eruptions pump millions of tons of gas and volcanic particles into the upper atmosphere. Volcanic clouds block some of the Sun's light and may temporarily lower temperatures on earth.

Mount Vesuvius left behind perfectly detailed molds of its victims.

An erupting volcano spews ash and debris into the atmosphere.

A helicopter stirs up a thick layer of ash deposited by an erupting volcano.

The year 1816 is sometimes referred to as "the year without a summer." The massive eruption of Tambora in Indonesia a year earlier led to dramatic weather events around the globe. The eruption was one of the largest in recorded history. The American northeast had wild temperature swings and summer snow. Lake and river ice was reported as far south as Pennsylvania in July and August. Red and brown snow, (believed to be caused by volcanic ash in the atmosphere) was reported in Europe. The cold weather caused widespread crop failure and food shortages.

Volcanologists hold shields to protect themselves from the heat.

DEADLY ERUPTIONS

One in ten people live near a potentially dangerous volcano, but even active volcanoes sometimes go hundreds of years between eruptions. Volcanoes can be deadly, but fortunately catastrophic eruptions are relatively rare.

Scientists estimate that roughly 200,000 people have lost their lives in volcanic eruptions in the last 500 years. By comparison, famine, earthquakes, and floods have killed millions. Volcanologists hope to have a reliable method for predicting eruptions. With advance warning, people can move away from danger.

A volcanologist takes measurements to detect earth that has moved or shifted.

Lahars from the Mount St. Helens eruption destroyed property miles from the volcano.

Lahars will swallow anything in their path.

Old faithful is a geyser—a hot spring that erupts—in Yellowstone National Park. The spring water is warmed as it flows over rock heated by magma deep below the earth's crust.

YELLOWSTONE

Yellowstone National Park sits atop one of the largest volcanic systems in the world. Scientists call it a **supervolcano**. In prehistoric times, the Yellowstone volcano erupted with unimaginable force, thousands of times more powerful than the recent eruption of Mount St. Helens. An eruption of this size in modern times could cause the **extinction** of many species including humans. Fortunately, scientists believe this type of eruption is not likely to occur in the next 100,000 years.

1985-Nevado del Ruiz, Columbia:

Erupting volcanoes can produce rivers of melted snow, mud, and volcanic debris. These giant mudflows are called lahars. In 1985, a lahar swept down the slopes of the Nevado del Ruiz volcano, devastating villages in its path. Twenty three thousand people were killed.

A CREATIVE FORCE

Today, visitors at the Windy Ridge overlook gaze across at Mount St. Helens roughly four miles away. The scarred landscape hints at what happened here in 1980. But the wounds from the eruption have already begun to heal. In fact, the recovery began as soon as the eruption ended. Wildlife has returned to the area. Flowers, trees, and other plants thrive in soil enriched by volcanic ash. New mountain lakes created by the eruption now support fish and other wildlife.

Volcanic eruptions are awesome forces of nature. They not only have the power to destroy, they also create. Volcanic eruptions have created some of the most beautiful and productive land on earth.

It may take years to fully recover, but Mount St. Helens will always be beautiful.

GLOSSARY

core (KOR) — the intensely hot center of the earth

crust (KRUHST) — the hard outer layer of the earth

dormant (DOR muhnt) — not currently active, but not
  yet extinct

eruption (ih RUHPT shuhn) — to spew forth volcanic debris

extinction (ek STINGKT shuhn) — the act of extinguishing

magma (MAG muh) — melted rock below the earth's surface

mantle (MAN tuhl) — the layer of the earth between the
  crust and core

molten (MOHLT un) — melted by heat

supervolcano (SOO per vol KAY no) — an enormous volcano

tectonic plates (tek TON ik PLAYT) — a piece of the
  earth's crust

FURTHER READING

Van Rose, Susanna. *Volcano & Earthquake.*
  DK Publishing, 2004.

Magloff, Lisa. *Volcano.* DK Publishing, 2003.

Simon, Seymour. *Volcanoes.* HarperCollins Publishers, 2006.

WEBSITES TO VISIT

FEMA For Kids
www.fema.gov/kids/volcano

USGS
http://volcanoes.usgs.gov/update.html

National Geographic
http://www.nationalgeographic.com/ngkids/0312/

INDEX

earthquakes   11
famine   24
flood   24
Hawaii   12, 15
Herculaneum   20
Kilauea   15
Krakatau   12
Nevado Del Ruiz   27
Mauna Loa   15
Mount Pinatubo   18, 19
Mount St. Helens   4, 7,
    27, 28
Mount Vesuvius   20
Olympus Mons   15

Pompeii   20
pyroclastic flow   8
Ring of Fire   8
supervolcano   27
Tambora   8, 23
Yellowstone   27

ABOUT THE AUTHORS

David and Patricia Armentrout have written many nonfiction books for young readers. They have had several books published for primary school reading. The Armentrouts live in Cincinnati, Ohio, with their two children.